Undaunted
Pandemic Prayers

*The Godly Woman's Devotional
and Prayer Journal*

Prudence Graham

rugged places a plain press

Undaunted Pandemic Prayers: The Godly Woman's Devotional and Prayer Journal

First edition. July, 2020.

Introduction

I'D ALWAYS ADMIRED Jane (not her real name). She was the kind of mom who seemed to do it all effortlessly. She was a little spitfire, no more than five feet tall. Our boys met in kindergarten, and Jane and I became school-mom friends, running into each other at back-to-school nights and on the soccer field. She had four kids altogether, but always managed to look put-together and throw the neighborhood's coolest summer party, complete with zip line that zoomed across her yard for the kids, and a patio-turned-dance-floor for tipsy neighbors to attempt a salsa dance or the latest line-dance moves.

A few years after I met her, Jane told me she was going back to nursing school. She had always been interested in healing, and it seemed like a logical choice for her. But as I saw how hard she had to work at it, I did wonder from time to time why she felt so called to it. She talked about the thick textbooks chock full of medical terms she had to memorize, and the exhausting hours of practice she had to put in at a local hospital. But Jane seemed to love it. Years later, she posted a proud picture of herself with her nursing certificate. She had made her dream come true.

When the pandemic hit, I wrote Jane a message. Our boys had gotten older and had begun to move in different circles, and without them being in school together, there was less of a chance that I'd bump into her. "How are you doing?" I wrote. "Is there anything I can do for you or the kids?"

It took her a few days for her to respond. At the time, our area was at its peak of infection, and she was working double shifts. Even in writing, she sounded exhausted. She wrote about how crazy the hospital was, and how awful it felt to see so many people so sick.

It was weeks before I learned that Jane had gotten sick herself. As with far too many people in our country, I experienced the fear, the frustration, the sadness. Having been widowed young, I know the pain of loss, and a familiar dread came over me. Jane was young, and healthy, and by all accounts she should be fine. Still, I couldn't shake my fear for her children and her husband. I prayed a lot for Jane. I'd like to say that my prayers saved her, but they didn't. God needed Jane home, and He took her there on a Tuesday, after nearly a month of her being on a ventilator and several times when it seemed like she just might pull through. She'd been healthy and active, full of dreams and hopes. But it was her time. As painful as it was for everyone, especially her young children, God called her home.

Jane's passing brought the pandemic home in ways that few other things could have. I loved her and admired her. She seemed to me like one of those people who would live to a ripe old age. Her passing challenged everything I believe about faith and about what it means to live in a fair and just world.

If you're like me, you are wondering why the terrible scourge of Covid-19 has come to our land. If you're like me, you're angry and frustrated and afraid. If you're like me, you've been asking God or answers. I have, day after day. What follows here is what I've found that brings solace and meaning during a challenging time.

We are forged in times such as this one. It's not only the pandemic challenging us now. It's a divided country, and people being unkind to one another, it's the economic stresses, it's the political upheaval. It is a frightening time to be alive. And, yet, God has a plan for you, for me, for our country. Even in these dark and difficult times, God is there, leading and guiding us. It may take a bit more effort than usual to hear Him, but, together, we can find our way in His light.

Please join me. The journey was never meant to be just easy or without challenge. God's people have been through far worse than this, and have left us a blessed document in the Scriptures, full of hope and guidance for these trying times. Let's take this time together to find our way in His word.

Here I offer you Pandemic Prayers.

How to use this book

WHETHER THE PANDEMIC has touched you personally, has harmed a loved one, or you want to draw closer to God in this frightening time, you will find solace, encouragement and hope here. There are twenty of my favorite Bible verses within these pages, with ruminations and thoughts, prayers and space for you to do your own work with them.

When you get to each new passage, take the time to read the passage and consider its meaning. One of the great powers of the Bible, given to us by God, is that while certain passages can seem deceptively simple at first reading, they reveal themselves in layer upon layer when you take time to reflect on them.

Take a passage a week if you want to delve deep into each concept presented. If you need a more concentrated approach, do a passage a day. In these trying times, listen to yourself and your own needs. If you work through this book quickly and still need more, take time to look at my longer, general-purpose **Undaunted: The Godly Woman's Devotional and Prayer Journal | God Walks with You Through the Valley and Lifts You Up a Confident Woman of Hope and Strength.**

God's word is here for us under all circumstances. It is in these trying times that we can find the most solace and the biggest growth in our faith, if we let God into our hearts and ask him to answer the questions we have. This book you hold is a tool to make it through difficult times a woman of greater hope, inspiration and faith.

Passage 1:

PHILIPPIANS 4:12-13

[12]I know how to be humbled, and I also know how to abound. In everything and in all things I have learned the secret both to be filled and to be hungry, both to abound and to be in need. [13] I can do all things through Christ, who strengthens me.

THOUGHTS ON THIS PASSAGE:

We begin with one of the most powerful passages in Scripture. This passage, taken from Paul's letter to the Philippians, gets to the heart of what many of us find challenging about these pandemic times: the fact that fortunes rise and fall so quickly and unexpectedly here on this earthly plane. "I know what it is to be in need, and I know what it is to have plenty."

Do you know what it is to be in need now? So many people are struggling these days. Some have been personally touched by this plague. Others have known financial insecurity. But even the fear of it, even if you have not personally been touched, can trigger memories of other times when you have known what it was like to be in need.

We would do anything to keep from having a loved one get sick, or having our families be in need. And, of course, we should do what we can to avoid those things, to the extend our human abilities can take on such massive things, bigger than ourselves.

But in this passage, we are reminded that the secret of being content in any and every situation is our relationship with God. It's why you're here, and why Scripture offers us so much during difficult times. It is moments like these in which we most need reminding that we can do all through God, even when it's difficult or scary.

———— ⟋⟍⟍⟍ ————

THIS WEEK'S PRAYER:

God, who has walked beside me when I've known need and when I've known plenty, keep me mindful of the secret of being content in every situation, that is, a path in Your light and love. Keep my eyes on my faith, and renew my heart, whether well fed or hungry, whether living in plenty or in want. I can do all through You, dear Lord, who give me strength and light my path, on this day and always.

———— ⟋⟍⟍⟍ ————

RUMINATIONS:

As you contemplate this week's passage, what are some ways in which you feel challenged today? It could be as simple as worrying that you won't get enough exercise under quarantine, or as life-altering as in facing the illness and impending death of a loved one. We seek God's strength in so many ways, and all are real and true. (As always, if you need more room, feel free to get an extra sheet of paper).

List them here. Lord, I need strength for:

_____

_____

_____

_____

_____

_____

_____

—————⟨∾⟩—————

WHAT ARE THREE WAYS you'll turn your pandemic concerns over to God today? Prayer? An act of kindness? A remote church service? List your ideas here:

_____

_____

_____

_____

_____

_____

_____

_____

_____

_____

_____

_____

_____

_____

_____

_____

_____

_____

_____

_____

Passage 2:

ROMANS 8:18

18For I consider that the sufferings of this present time are not worthy to be compared with the glory which will be revealed to us.

THOUGHTS ON THIS PASSAGE:

Perspective. It's challenging even under the easiest of circumstances. And these are the opposite of easy circumstances.

It is sometimes difficult for us, as mortals, to understand the scope and breadth of God's view of life and the world. How can we expect to understand the sweeping view of He who created everything and has lived forever? Understandably, we see things from our limited view, in relationship to the scope of our earthly life. That is normal, and right, because that's the experience we are having currently.

However, it helps to ask God to help us remember the broader scope of the glories we have yet to see revealed or to experience. This is not intended to say we should not care about our health or that of our loved ones, or our troubles and those of our loved ones. Of course we should! The things that we're experiencing here and now are real and our feelings about them are real. It's just that one way to cope with the uncertainty and fear of these pandemic days is to lift our eyes to our broader, eternal life. We are eternal, spiritual beings having a human experience. The more we can remember to ask God to remind us of the coming glories, the more perspective we'll have on our current troubles.

This week's prayer:

Dear God, when I struggle, when I am in fear, help me find solace in the glory that will be revealed to me. Although I know all things happen on Your time and in Your way, help me stay peaceful and joyful that I am in Your hand through hard times and good times.

———— ⚬⦿⚬ ————

RUMINATIONS:

Think about fears you've had in the past, which did not come to pass. I'm talking about the relationships you thought you couldn't live without, only to find that letting them go was the best thing for you. The job you lost, only to find a better one.

This is not to play down the real fears we're all feeling. It's only to take a moment to take stock that sometimes our fears do not come true in the ways we dread. This is a first step to remembering that even in suffering we can focus on the glories ahead, even if we can't yet see them. List a few examples here:

_____

_____

_____

_____

_____

_____

_____

———— ⚬⦿⚬ ————

WHAT ARE THREE WAYS God has give you unexpected gifts? Things that looked bad at first, but turned out to have unexpected good consequences? See if you can list three:

_____

_____

_____

Passage 3:

PROVERBS 18:10

¹⁰The name of the Lord is a fortified tower;
the righteous run to it and are safe.

THOUGHTS ON THIS PASSAGE:

There have been few times in our living memory when we needed the safety and security of God more than we do now. The national news is alarming, both health-wise and economically. This is the defining moment of our generation, the grand challenge we will remember and talk about all the rest of our lives.

As with every challenge, there's the specifics of it, and there's also how we meet the moment. We've all grown up with stories about how previous generations have handled great adversities. Maybe you have heard of relatives who lived through the Great Depression and then kept cash under the mattress for the rest of their lives. And certainly you've heard of the Greatest Generation, who confronted the trials of World War II with such grace and courage. This is such a moment for us. We can choose fear, or we can choose to focus on our faith and grow through it. When we remember God is like our fortified tower, what great mercy and courage are we capable of?

THIS WEEK'S PRAYER:

God, keep me mindful of the fact that You are my fortified tower, my safety, my rock, my source of inspiration and solace. When times are difficult, when I am afraid, help me run to You and be safe as I weather this storm.

———— ⚬◦⚬ ————

RUMINATIONS:

What good is a fortified tower if you don't take refuge in it? Every time we let fear take us, we don't make use of the great and steady safety that God provides.

There's no judgement in this. These are difficult times, and we are flawed and human. Still, part of growing in our faith during this difficult time is learning to turn all our troubles over to God. Make a list here of your biggest "what if" concerns about the pandemic, the economic fallout and other things in your life that currently worry you:

_____

_____

_____

_____

_____

_____

_____

———— ⚬◦⚬ ————

WHAT WOULD YOUR LIFE look like if you were fully able to turn your worries over to God? What might you do different? I'm not talking about being less careful, of course, because one of the tools God gives us in these trying times is our sense and the guidance of medical experts. I'm talking about your inner life. How might you be more at peace if you allowed yourself to be fully aware of God's presence in your life? How might you get more creative about meeting your own needs during this trying time? List a few ideas here:

Passage 4:

DEUTERONOMY 31:6

⁶Be strong and courageous. Don't be afraid or scared of them; for the Lord your God himself is who goes with you. He will not fail you nor forsake you.

THOUGHTS ON THIS PASSAGE:

This is a time that calls for much strength and courage. However, it is at just such a time that strength and courage sometimes feels like they're at their lowest supply.

Fortunately, God is eternal and always there for us. Even if we've been afraid and not tapping in to the supply of strength and courage He has at the ready for us, we can change that on a moment's notice, any day we choose to. That is to say, even if you've been having a hard time finding the strength and courage in God, no matter how hard you've tried, you can still do it today. All you need do is ask. He will never leave you nor forsake you, no matter how frightening the world around you is right now.

THIS WEEK'S PRAYER:

God, please teach me to be strong and courageous in the face of all adversities. In my darkest moments I've been afraid, even terrified. I know that You are with me in all things, so I humbly ask for the faith and the focus to remember this and turn my worries and fears over to You, my Lord, who are all-powerful and always with me.

RUMINATIONS:

Perfect faith means perfect peace. But perfect faith is hard, and even more so in times of strife or worry. The Lord understands this, and is always there to remind us that He will never leave us or forsake us.

Sometimes, finding our strength comes easier when we think of others we need to be strong for. That's not to say we should neglect our own self-care. Instead, it means that when we see each other as part of a collective, we sometimes feel the call to more fully tap into God's courage.

For whom do you want to be strong during these pandemic times? The answer could be obvious, like children or a spouse. But if you live alone, you're still needed and important. It could be something as simple as staying strong for the people you meet casually in your daily life, or for your co-workers or church members. List those people here:

_____

_____

_____

_____

_____

_____

_____

HOW CAN YOU CALL ON God to give you courage to fully support these people during this difficult time? Again, it could be simple, like sending an email of encouragement, or it could be big, like committing to leaving prepared meals outside the homes of infected family members. List a few ideas here, then incorporate those requests into your prayers:

_____

Passage 5:

JAMES 5:15

[15]and the prayer of faith will heal him who is sick, and the Lord will raise him up. If he has committed sins, he will be forgiven.

THOUGHTS ON THIS PASSAGE:

God reminds us again and again that prayer is powerful and important. Especially during these scary times, this passage of Scripture gives me great solace. "Prayer offered in faith will make the sick person well."

Studies show the power of prayer. Of course, it bears repeating, this is not to mean that we should forsake the power of medicine or that we should stop listening to experts. Among the many ways God responds to our prayers is by sending us the right doctors and medicines to overcome this scourge. Still, a calm and prayerful mind can make a great difference for yourself, your family, and your community. Now more than ever, refocusing on offering prayers in faith can make a great difference for yourself and others.

THIS WEEK'S PRAYER:

God, above all I pray to make the sick people well. There is great suffering in my community and my land, and I beseech you to give me the faith to strengthen the power of my prayers, joining mine with the many faithful who are also seeking strength from you right now. Magnify the power of my prayers, join my voices with the faithful, and help us bring a swift end to the suffering of our land.

———— ⚬ ————

RUMINATIONS:

Prayer. It is important always, but especially during challenging times. Of course you know that, which is why you invested in this book and in all the other ways you work to recommit to your faith. It matters now more than ever to lift your voice up to God and ask for His intersession and guidance.

Too often we think we need "perfect" conditions for prayer. We may be feeling cut off from our community if in-person church services have been suspended in our communities. We may even feel resentful of that, and concerned that it interferes with our connection to God.

Of course, God is everywhere and in all things. Although there is something special about praying in church, truly we can find Him everywhere and in all things, big and small. Think of some new ways to incorporate prayer into your everyday moments. Can you give a small prayer of thanks as you prepare your family's food? For your health as you walk? Can you wake up a bit earlier, before everyone else, to spend some time in prayer? List some ideas here:

_____

_____

_____

_____

_____

_____

_____

———— ⚬ ————

WHO WOULD YOU LIKE to pray for this week? Family members, leaders, sick people in your community? Make a list of people to keep in your prayers. Update this list weekly or daily as needed:

_____

_____

_____

_____

_____

_____

_____

_____

_____

_____

_____

_____

_____

_____

_____

_____

_____

_____

_____

_____

_____

_____

_____

_____

Passage 6:

MARK 12:29-31

29"The most important one," answered Jesus, "is this: 'Hear, O Israel: The Lord our God, the Lord is one. 30Love the Lord your God with all your heart and with all your soul and with all your mind and with all your strength.' 31The second is this: 'Love your neighbor as yourself.' There is no commandment greater than these."

THOUGHTS ON THIS PASSAGE:

The Golden Rule. If you're like most of us, you grew up on it. It's perfect in its simplicity. What would a world look like in which we truly all loved our neighbors as we love ourselves? What would life be like if we extended the same level of care to others as we do our own family? It would mean the end of wars and fighting neighbors. It would mean intact families. It would be glorious.

As with so many concepts of Scripture, it is okay to recognize the ways in which this is an ideal and something we have to keep trying to strive for. Loving others as we love ourselves is hard. When things are challenging, as they are right now, it's even harder. But, as this passage of Scripture says, "there is no commandment greater." First is to love God, of course. And right beside that, the call to love our neighbor as ourselves.

THIS WEEK'S PRAYER:

Merciful God, I hear your words and I strive to know Your will. I love You with all my heart, my soul, my mind and all my strength, which I know derives from You. I ask for your guidance, in these dark days, to love my neighbor as myself, even when it's hard, even when I am afraid and concerned about the actions of others. Fill me with Your love and understanding and help me love my fellow humans as You love all your children.

RUMINATIONS:

Unconditional love is difficult under the best of circumstances. We strive for it but sometimes fail to reach it even with the people we love best. We even fail to love our own selves unconditionally at times, even though we know our own hearts better than anyone else's.

This need to love others as we love ourselves is especially difficult in these pandemic days, when others are behaving in ways we don't understand. Whether you're frustrated by neighbors who aren't social distancing as you are, or by social media acquaintances posting things you find objectionable or even abhorrent, it is hard to love right now. And yet loving our neighbors as ourselves is what God calls us to do. As with all of God's guidance, it isn't just for when things are easy, but especially for when things are hard.

Below, list some people you are finding it hard to love right now. If those people may stumble on this book and you don't want to cause further strife, you can write the list on a separate sheet of paper you later discard, or on a Note in your phone. The idea is to become aware of where you are failing to love your neighbor as yourself. Not just the "easy" neighbors, either, and, of course, not just "neighbors," but all our fellow humans.

_____

_____

_____

_____

_____

_____

_____

——— ೧ల ———

CAN YOU HOLD THE PEOPLE on the list above in your prayers?
Yes, it's hard to pray for those we find challenging. But as someone who
knows the power of prayer, it is the greatest gift you can give in the effort to become a more perfect and loving follower of Christ. Write about
your commitment to love your neighbor as yourself, even when it's hard:

_____

_____

_____

_____

_____

_____

_____

_____

_____

_____

_____

_____

_____

_____

_____

_____

_____

_____

_____

_____

_____

_____

Passage 7:

ISAIAH 40:29

^{29}He gives strength to the weary
and increases the strength of him who has no might.

THOUGHTS ON THIS PASSAGE:

The length and ferocity of this pandemic has made us all weary. We are weary of spirit and, some of us, weary of body as well. It is a natural reaction to this trying national moment.

It is in the moments when we're most weary and weak that God is there for us in His greatest fullness. We must find ways to notice and note our weakness and weariness, and turn it over to God to turn into strength and power.

This is sometimes easier said than done. It is our nature as women to want to push on and try harder, to care for everyone else before we care for ourselves. It is an honorable and good instinct that many of us have, but we can't let it keep us from taking the time we need to let God recharge and reenergize us. There is no shame in needing to ask for strength when we're feeling weak, and in following God's guidance to recharge our energy when it's necessary.

THIS WEEK'S PRAYER:

Dear God, I am grateful for all the gifts You give me, and for the many ways I am blessed even in these difficult days. Lord, sometimes I am weary, and I feel weak. I ask that you help me open to your strength and power. I ask, too, Lord, that you help me get more attuned to when I'm giving too much or putting too much of a strain on myself, so that I can stop to refresh myself with prayer and retreat where I can, so that I may be strengthened and empowered by Your word.

RUMINATIONS:

Self-care is not always top of mind when things are hard. There are things to get done! People to cook for, things to do. But God knows us better than anyone, and will give us signals to relax, unwind and ask for help when we need it. A limitless supply of God's strength and power is available to us if we tap in, ask, and allow ourselves to receive. This takes contemplation and time to be with God. While it's tempting to just go-go-go, we also need silence and peace to make it through this tough time.

What are some ways in which you're stretching yourself too thin? How can you be more compassionate with yourself about it? Write your worries to God here, and ask for messages about how to receive strength and power through Him:

_____

_____

_____

_____

_____

_____

_____

Is there a friend or family member whom you also notice is stretching herself too thin? Someone always ready with a casserole or always trying to save the day? Can you be a force in helping her find some rest and peace? We need quiet and regrouping now. Write a letter to a friend about your wishes for their peace and ease. You can decide whether or not to send it after you take a moment to get the thoughts down:

_____

_____

_____

_____

_____

_____

_____

_____

_____

_____

_____

_____

_____

_____

_____

_____

_____

_____

_____

_____

_____

_____

_____

_____

Passage 8:

PSALM 146:8

⁸ the Lord gives sight to the blind,
the Lord lifts up those who are bowed down,
the Lord loves the righteous.

THOUGHTS ON THIS PASSAGE:

Here, Scripture quite literally means that God is capable of healing all things, including giving sight to the blind. No infirmity is too great for God. We've all heard stories about the miraculous power of prayer, and of people being healed even though doctors were sure that there was nothing more to be done.

But, for a moment, I want to spend some time talking about the symbolic meaning of blindness. While God can return physical sight to a person who has lost it, one of God's greatest miracles is giving us the ability to see things we've missed before. To face difficult truths. To undertake difficult self-examination, or a review of our relationships or other life conditions.

This pandemic has been frightening and life-altering. If you or someone you know has gotten sick, you know what this virus can do better than most. But even if you've managed to stay out of the maw of this killer, the global upheaval is frightening and unsettling. However, it is in times like this when we can open ourselves up to see truths we've missed before. They may be challenging, or unpleasant, but looking at things clearly always yields good results. It can also bring us closer to God by causing the scales to fall from our eyes.

———— ⟲⟳ ————

THIS WEEK'S PRAYER:

Lord, show me the ways I've been blind, lift me up and teach me righteousness and piety. I strive every day to live in truth and self-reflection, and I ask for Your blessed help on my journey. In this difficult time, I ask for your clarity and strength most of all.

———— ⟲⟳ ————

RUMINATIONS:

Spend some time thinking about the ways this pandemic has illuminated truths about your life. For some, good things have come to the surface. Families have grown closer despite the need to socially distance, getting creative, scheduling more Zoom calls, and otherwise finding ways to express love for one another. Other truths have been tougher to cope with: the neighbor who isn't being as careful as you'd want them to be, the mate who is more difficult to deal with in quarantine, the job that seems more precarious (or is gone now). What are some difficult truths these hard days have revealed to you?

_____

_____

_____

_____

_____

_____

_____

What do you need from God to fully open yourself to the reality of your situation? What comes next after having your "blindness" revealed to you? Do you need to work on your marriage? Upgrade your skills to find a new job? Take the plunge and start that online business you've been scared to try? What is God showing you that you need to do differently? While these are scary times, we can emerge stronger, more godly and more bonded to God if we use this adversity to grow. Write your thoughts here:

_____

_____

_____

_____

_____

_____

_____

_____

_____

_____

_____

_____

_____

_____

_____

_____

_____

_____

_____

_____

_____

Passage 9:

JAMES 4:8

[8]Come near to God and he will come near to you. Wash your hands, you sinners, and purify your hearts.

THOUGHTS ON THIS PASSAGE:

"Wash your hands." How many times have you heard that in the last few months? If you're like me: a lot. But here it is straight from Scripture: wash your hands.

Of course, this passage is about more than physical hand-washing, although the reminder of good hygiene is welcome and necessary. It is about purifying our hearts and drawing nearer to God.

In this context, washing your hands means making yourself free of deeds that make you unclean. Use your hands for good things so that you may feel them clean. Purifying your heart is about examining your motivations and the kindness of your thoughts, and striving always to draw nearer to God. He knows we are sinners by nature, and he gives us endless chances to "wash our hands" and purify our hearts. When we step nearer to God, He steps nearer to us. We need that now more than ever.

THIS WEEK'S PRAYER:

Beloved God, show me always how to constantly draw nearer to you in word, thought and deed. Wash me clean, purify my heart, and guide me in Your ways so that I may speak kind thoughts, think positive, caring thoughts and do good deeds every moment of my life. If I falter, help me admit my wrongs and find my way to Your forgiveness so that I can live up to the ideals of a life in Christ.

RUMINATIONS:

What habits make you feel "clean" inside? Perhaps it's as small as saying a kind word to a neighbor about their garden over the fence. Perhaps it's as big as calling your parents and telling them the great difference they've made in your life. There are kindnesses, big and small, which bring us nearer to the people who we want to be. When we draw nearer to God in this way, by being the kind of believer that acts in good and wholesome ways, God also draws nearer to us. Think of three such actions you can take today. Try to list things you don't normally already do. The idea is to add on to your good habits:

_____

_____

_____

_____

_____

_____

WHAT SINS ARE YOU CARRYING around inside you? Sometimes, no matter how hard we work to cleanse our hearts, good deeds aren't enough. We need to admit our sins to God, ask for forgiveness, and strive to do better. This is hard for us all. But the power of it is unmistakable. List three heavy things you've been carrying in your heart, and ask God for the insight into what it will take to finally put the burdens of your sins down. As with other items, it's okay to write on a separate sheet if you're more comfortable with that.

_____

_____

_____

_____

_____

_____

_____

_____

_____

_____

_____

_____

_____

_____

_____

_____

_____

_____

_____

_____

_____

_____

_____

Passage 10:

EXODUS 23:25

²⁵Worship the Lord your God, and his blessing will be on your food and water. I will take away sickness from among you.

THOUGHTS ON THIS PASSAGE:

At first blush, this may look like a passage about asking for God's blessing on your food. And it can be. If you're in the habit of saying grace before a meal, you know its transformative power, the feeling of gratitude that can turn even a simple meal into a feast from God.

But in the context of this pandemic, and any health crisis, this passage means something more. It is a reminder to take good care of your body and nourish it with good, clean, nutritious food.

If you've read **Undaunted: The Godly Woman's Devotional and Prayer Journal | God Walks with You Through the Valley and Lifts You Up a Confident Woman of Hope and Strength** you may recall the passage about your body being a temple in which the Holy Spirit lives, and what our responsibilities are in taking care of that temple.

In the context of a pandemic, the focus on good food and clean water becomes additional call to take care of the temple that is your body. Of course no one is saying that simply by eating your veggies can you keep Covid-19 away, but that in giving your body all the right building blocks, you give yourself the tools to stay as healthy as you can. As always, follow the guidance of medical professionals and maintain your quarantine and social distancing protocols as experts recommend. But, also, be extra good to your body. Walk in the fresh air if you can. Say grace over your food, and pick meals that are nutritious.

This sickness will one day be taking from among us. It is our jobs to stay as healthy as we reasonably can as we make it through.

———— ❧ ————

THIS WEEK'S PRAYER:

Almighty God, I worship you in all things, and thank you for the abundance and blessings that You provide me. I ask for Your blessings on my food and water, and Your guidance in choosing healthful, nourishing foods that give my body strength to serve you, care for my family, and remain as healthy as You will it. Although I know Your plans are beyond my human understanding, I ask that you take this sickness away from among us, on Your timing and according to Your will, and that you give me the strength to withstand what I must. All this I ask in Jesus' blessed name.

———— ❧ ————

RUMINATIONS:

Think a moment about your eating habits. This can be a topic full of a lifetime of frustration and disappointment, especially if you've struggled with your weight, had a critical parent, or have health issues. Try, if you can to put those things aside. Think instead of your body as a temple that requires certain things, and clean fuel (food) is among those things. Have you been eating well? Exercising (in a socially distant way, of course)? Getting enough rest. Write an honest assessment of the kind of care you've been taking of your body since the pandemic started. As always, use an extra sheet if you need it:

———— ❧ ————

_____

_____

_____

_____

_____

_____

_____

WITH THE ABOVE ASSESSMENT in mind, take a moment to think of three habits you can add to start moving in a healthier direction. Is there one snack that is your "weakness" and which you can resolve to no longer keep in your pantry? Can you get up a bit earlier (or stay up a bit later) and go out for a walk? List at least three new habits you'll try this week. And then stick to it!

_____

_____

_____

_____

_____

_____

_____

_____

_____

_____

_____

_____

_____

_____

_____

_____

_____

_____

_____

_____

_____

_____

Passage 11:

MARK 6:56

⁵⁶And wherever he went—into villages, towns or countryside—they placed the sick in the marketplaces. They begged him to let them touch even the edge of his cloak, and all who touched it were healed.

THOUGHTS ON THIS PASSAGE:

This is perhaps one of best-known images of Jesus, that of healer. When he went into villages, towns or the countryside, the sick were placed in marketplaces. Even by touching the edge of his cloak, all who drew near were healed. So amazing is the power of Christ!

Today, we don't have the blessing of being able to touch Jesus' cloak. But we have other ways to access His blessings and mercy. One of the most powerful is with prayer, which is what we're studying here together.

How can we "touch the cloak" of Jesus, so to speak? It's about drawing close and believing in His word. As I've said in other parts of this book, an investment in faith means also being mindful of the worldly techniques God gives us: staying vigilant in our mask-wearing and handwashing, for example, and heeding the advice of experts. But it also means drawing nearer to Jesus in thought and word and deed, now more than ever. And reveling in the glory of the work of Jesus when He walked among us is a powerful reminder of what true faith can bring.

THIS WEEK'S PRAYER:

Dear Jesus, who helped the sick and brought Your love into this world, please guide me in staying healthy and safe during these uncertain times, and bring Your healing to our world as you did to all who touched your cloak in villages and in the countryside. Shine Your love on us once more.

———— ⚬ ————

RUMINATIONS:

Reading Scripture is one of my great solaces. This week, take a moment to look up some of Jesus' most meaningful acts of healing. Here are a few recommended passages:

Matthew 8

Luke 8:40

Mark 2

John 9

Read and re-read these passages. Think about how they might apply to our current situation. Make a list of the health issues you want to turn over to God. Then listen for guidance in your prayers.

———— ⚬ ————

_____

_____

_____

_____

_____

_____

THINK OF WAYS YOU CAN incorporate the stories of Jesus healing the sick into your days. Would it be helpful to read one each day? To discuss it with a prayer group over Zoom? To write a note of thanks to God each day for His many blessings? Try this last idea below to see if it resonates with you:

_____

_____

_____

_____

_____

_____

_____

_____

_____

_____

_____

_____

_____

_____

_____

_____

_____

_____

_____

_____

_____

_____

_____

_____

_____

Passage 12:

JOHN 16:22

²²So with you: Now is your time of grief, but I will see you again and you will rejoice, and no one will take away your joy.

THOUGHTS ON THIS PASSAGE:

This is a time of national grief. Whether this pandemic has hit you personally, or a loved one, or whether you just watch what's happening on the news and mourn, it is a difficult time. This passage in John reminds us that grief comes into each life.

There is a certain solace in this difficult knowledge. No one wants grief, and sometimes it feels too big to bear. But it is part of the human experience. Taking a longer view and understanding that there are times of grief, and times of rejoicing, helps us remember that this too shall pass.

And, most importantly, it is critical to remember that when we have joys, no one can take them away.

THIS WEEK'S PRAYER:

God, help me find strength in You during this time of grief. Keep my eyes raised above any given moment and to the larger mission of living a good, Christian life here on Earth. Help keep my spirits up until we reach a time of joy, and help me remember the ultimate joy, which is everlasting.

--------- ❦ ---------

RUMINATIONS:

Although the passage above refers to the everlasting joy, it is powerful to remember that what we focus on stays with us. Even during difficult times, joys are things that can uplift us and remind us that better days are coming. When things are especially hard, we may need to work hard to find the joys. For example, one sick friend who was hospitalized recently told me that the joy of speaking to grandchildren via FaceTime meant the difference between a good day and a bad one. Even something as simple as a new magazine can be a source of great joy when other things feel dire.

What are some joys no one can take away from you? No matter how small, list them here. Dig deep into the simple things you can feel gratitude for:

--------- ❦ ---------

_____

_____

_____

_____

_____

_____

_____

JOYFUL RITUALS. SOMETIMES joys are things we can create for ourselves. You're probably doing this in some ways already, but being more mindful of it can emphasize the joy. Psychologists call this savoring, that is, the conscious act of noticing the small, good things and incorporating more of them into your life. What small rituals can you create (or notice more) that bring you joy? If you're well, perhaps time in the garden, or a walk in nature, or even using your favorite mug when you make a special cup of tea you enjoy mindfully? If you're unwell, perhaps it's the small moments of respite or comfort or kindness. List some ideas here:

_____

_____

_____

_____

_____

_____

_____

_____

_____

_____

_____

_____

_____

_____

_____

_____

_____

_____

_____

_____

_____

_____

_____

Passage 13:

JAMES 1:2-3

[2]Consider it pure joy, my brothers and sisters,[a1] whenever you face trials of many kinds, [3]because you know that the testing of your faith produces perseverance.

THOUGHTS ON THIS PASSAGE:

This is a tough one for me, which is all the more reason why I need to pray on it and sit with it more than most. I don't like tests. I don't like pain. I don't like sadness and fear, all of which are in ample supply during these uncertain times. I want to be a stronger, more devout person, but I am human, and I want ease and comfort too.

It has been a lifetime pattern for me that when I see a trial, my first reaction is to pull away from it. If you've studying life and Scripture as long as I have, you must also know that this only serves to prolong the trial, and make the lesson harder to learn.

This passage sets a high and important standard when faced with adversity. Imagine if we could learn to consider them pure joys? When we truly understand that the testing of our faith makes us persevere, we can open our hearts to seeing the pure joy in adversity. I'm not saying this is easy. It certainly isn't for me! But every time I've been able to appreciate

---

1.   https://www.biblegateway.com/passage/?search=James+1%3A2-3&version=NIV#fen-NIV-30269a

the opportunity for growth in a test of faith, I have grown more resilient and I have learned better what it means to persevere. Here, God calls us to welcome these opportunities with pure joy.

THIS WEEK'S PRAYER:

Mighty God, I look to you and ask that you help me open my heart to the pure joy of growing in my faith and in my goal of becoming a better, stronger person. Help me learn to welcome tests of my faith and expand my capacity to persevere not just for myself, but for Your church and all the world.

RUMINATIONS:

What trials are you facing right now? Sometimes there's comfort in just acknowledging what those are. No trial is too small, and, of course, putting the biggest ones into words might help the most. Is someone you love sick? Are you worried about what happens next? Are you financially insecure right now? Are you heartsick at the unkindness you see around you? List your trials here:

_____

_____

_____

_____

_____

_____

HOW WILL GOING THROUGH these trials increase your perseverance and your faith? List some ideas here:

_____

_____

_____

_____

_____

_____

_____

_____

_____

_____

_____

_____

_____

_____

_____

_____

_____

_____

_____

_____

_____

_____

_____

_____

Passage 14:

PROVERBS 26:20

²⁰ Without wood a fire goes out;
without a gossip a quarrel dies down.

THOUGHTS ON THIS PASSAGE:

Where do you get your information about the pandemic? If you're like a lot of us, social media is at least a part of that. And if you're like me, you've seen a lot of things posted back and forth, people digging into their positions, and unkind memes and words being thrown in all directions. And, sometimes, even well-meaning friends pass on misinformation and things which inflame others.

Scripture is clear on this type of behavior: don't engage in it. Here is but one of a multitude of passages that warn against passing on dubious information. The image is simple: if there's no wood (gossip), then there is no quarrel. At this difficult time in our lives, quarrels can be a fire that rages out of control.

A godly person is not one who scolds and tries to shout louder than the rest, although it can be tempting when we are sure of our version of the truth. But it is not as Jesus would have done when He walked among us, and it is not helpful.

In these trying times, it's important to keep to reputable, reliable sources of information: doctors, experts, and public health experts. We can reduce our intake of information simply to what we need to keep ourselves and our families healthy: what do we need to know nationally to slow down the spread? What do we need to know locally, things like where is it safe to shop or what parks or establishments are open or closed? Beyond that, all the speculation and flame throwing doesn't serve us or the greater good. Let's keep our eyes on God.

———— ⟋⟍⟍ ————

THIS WEEK'S PRAYER:

God, help me be the faithful who doesn't feed fuel to the fire, or gossip to quarrels. Help me keep my eyes on peace and healing, and wash me clean of all anger and resentment. Help me bask in the pure, clear water of Your Word and revel only in truth.

———— ⟋⟍⟍ ————

RUMINATIONS:

We face twin challenges: the health crisis that is in our country, and the words that are flying back and forth about it. We are too small to affect the first one, save to do what we can to keep ourselves and our loved ones safe. But we have much power over how we engage in the second.

Here, list some sources of information that have caused you strife and maybe even anger in the last few weeks. Has it been a particularly vocal family member on social media? An especially inflammatory source of news? Make an inventory:

_____
_____
_____
_____
_____
_____

Now, what are some ways you can create some distance between yourself and the source of gossip or strife? If it's a family member on social media, are you close enough to tell them how their posts are affecting you? If you're not, are you comfortable muting their posts, at least for a short while? Can you limit your media intake to a certain amount of time per day? In what ways can you be the kind of person that doesn't add wood to the fire? List your ideas here:

_____

_____

_____

_____

_____

_____

_____

_____

_____

_____

_____

_____

_____

_____

_____

_____

_____

_____

_____

_____

Passage 15:

MATTHEW 6:25-32

25 Therefore I tell you, do not worry about your life, what you will eat or drink; or about your body, what you will wear. Is not life more than food, and the body more than clothes? 26 Look at the birds of the air; they do not sow or reap or store away in barns, and yet your heavenly Father feeds them.

THOUGHTS ON THIS PASSAGE:

Financial worries. "Safety" worries. This scourge of the coronavirus brings with it much more than just concerns about one's health and the health of loved ones and of everyone in our country. With record unemployment, businesses shut down, lowered consumer confidence and uncertainty about when we'll get back to normal, it is reasonable to feel concern about the financial future (and present!).

But as with all things that trouble us, the solution is always to turn it over to God. I make sure to make the distinction that turning issues over to God does not equal inaction. Instead, we enter into an active dialogue with God. We pray, we request, and then we get quiet and listen for the many ways that God answers our prayers. Opportunities. Thoughts of an old co-worker who is at a new company where you want to try and get a job. That quiet voice that tells you to finally go for starting that business you've been dreaming about for a long time.

Knowing God will provide is about partnering with God and boldly acting on the signs He sends you.

THIS WEEK'S PRAYER:

God, my life is Yours, my spirit and mind and heart are yours. Take away my worries about what my family and loved ones and I will eat or drink or wear. Let me be like the birds in the air, confident in Your ever-plentiful supply of sustenance. Help me be like the fish that swim and keep alert for every opportunity. Give me the strength and cleverness to be resourceful, and keep my heart calm so that I may weather this difficult time.

RUMINATIONS:

Financial worries. Just about everyone has them these days. Those of us that have jobs worry they'll go away. Those of us that don't wonder how we'll find another. The challenges are real and not to be minimized. But by making an inventory, we can begin to get a handle on all that is troubling you. Make a list of your financial worries, especially any related to changes that have happened due to the pandemic:

_____

_____

_____

_____

_____

_____

_____

Listening. Hearing God's guidance takes practice and faith. Take a moment to pray on the worries you listed above. Ask God specifically to show you the path forward. Then make a list of all the ideas that come into your mind, no matter how far-fetched or impractical they may feel.

For the next week, pay special attention to what you hear, see online or in the entertainment you consume, or read. Seek out free podcasts and articles on things that interest you or worry you. For example, if you get the inkling that one way forward is to finally start that online business, seek out podcasts on starting a business with a low initial investment. Don't be "sure" anything is the right answer. This is about staying open-minded and opening yourself up to guidance. List your ideas here. Make this a living list that you add to as new ideas and insights come to you. Use an additional piece of paper, or maybe even dedicate a notebook to these ideas:

_____

_____

_____

_____

_____

_____

_____

_____

_____

_____

_____

_____

_____

_____

_____

_____

_____

_____

_____

_____

_____

_____

Passage 16:

PROVERBS 19:20-21

20 Listen to advice and accept discipline,
and at the end you will be counted among the wise.

21 Many are the plans in a person's heart,
but it is the Lord's purpose that prevails.

THOUGHTS ON THIS PASSAGE:

I like to pair this passage with the one we focused on last week because, to me, they are two sides of a coin. Last week's passage was about trusting in God to provide, but doing so actively, with an open mind as to what you must to do find your way through this difficult time.

This one gives us a backbone of hard work and discipline to that trust. It is not simply enough to say your prayers and not listen to what God demands of you. God speaks to us in many ways, including in the wise words of those who have done the things we hope to do, who tell us of the discipline and rigor required to reach our goals. In other words, as an example, it is not simply enough to ask God to get you a new job. We must get feedback on our resumes, reach out to everyone we know, take constructive criticism and prepare for any interview that comes our way. We must listen to advice and accept discipline. The road to wisdom is long and requires a lot of learning.

I particularly like this passage because I am the type of person that gets very swept up in my excitement when I think I know the path to take. For example, when I prayed and it was revealed to me that I should take my hand-written devotionals and share them with others, I wanted to jump right into it. But as I learned and listened, I discovered that creating a book like the one you hold in your hands (or in your device!) requires a lot of work I had no idea about: graphic design, typesetting, marketing help. I spent years learning the craft of book creation, in addition to crafting the message of these devotionals. If I'd gone off as my instincts encouraged me to, these books probably wouldn't have reached all the people they have. Just because a plan is in your heart, it doesn't mean you don't have to do the work to make it real. And, above all, understand that it is the Lord's purpose that prevails. When things don't happen as we want them to, the Lord has different and better plans for us. It is about staying open, learning from our mistakes, and moving forward with a joyful heart.

THIS WEEK'S PRAYER:

Beloved God, help me grow in wisdom and humility, to listen to advice and accept discipline. It is my life's goal to be counted among the wise, but I know how long and arduous a path that is, so I seek out experts and advisors to keep growing and learning. There are many plans in my heart, but I know it is Your purpose that prevails, and I open joyfully to learn of your plans for me.

RUMINATIONS:

What plans are in your heart? It may be hard to focus on them now, but it helps our hearts and minds to look at the bigger picture and remember. Whether it's finally writing that memoir, or simply starting a "side hustle" to cover unexpected pandemic-related expenses, take a moment to take stock of what you want to accomplish:

_____

_____

_____

_____

_____

What do I need to do to listen to advice and accept discipline? Who has achieved what I'm hoping to do, and how can I learn from them? Are they friends and co-workers I can call, or experts whose articles and videos I can watch? Brainstorm some ideas:

_____

_____

_____

_____

_____

_____

_____

_____

_____

_____

_____

_____

_____

_____

_____

_____

_____

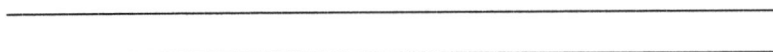

Passage 17:

PROVERBS 19:20-21

²⁰ Listen to advice and accept discipline,
and at the end you will be counted among the wise.

²¹ Many are the plans in a person's heart,
but it is the Lord's purpose that prevails.

THOUGHTS ON THIS PASSAGE:

I like to pair this passage with the one we focused on last week because, to me, they are two sides of a coin. Last week's passage was about trusting in God to provide, but doing so actively, with an open mind as to what you must to do find your way through this difficult time.

This one gives us a backbone of hard work and discipline to that trust. It is not simply enough to say your prayers and not listen to what God demands of you. God speaks to us in many ways, including in the wise words of those who have done the things we hope to do, who tell us of the discipline and rigor required to reach our goals. In other words, as an example, it is not simply enough to ask God to get you a new job. We must get feedback on our resumes, reach out to everyone we know, take constructive criticism and prepare for any interview that comes our way. We must listen to advice and accept discipline. The road to wisdom is long and requires a lot of learning.

I particularly like this passage because I am the type of person that gets very swept up in my excitement when I think I know the path to

57

take. For example, when I prayed and it was revealed to me that I should take my hand-written devotionals and share them with others, I wanted to jump right into it. But as I learned and listened, I discovered that creating a book like the one you hold in your hands (or in your device!) requires a lot of work I had no idea about: graphic design, typesetting, marketing help. I spent years learning the craft of book creation, in addition to crafting the message of these devotionals. If I'd gone off as my instincts encouraged me to, these books probably wouldn't have reached all the people they have. Just because a plan is in your heart, it doesn't mean you don't have to do the work to make it real. And, above all, understand that it is the Lord's purpose that prevails. When things don't happen as we want them to, the Lord has different and better plans for us. It is about staying open, learning from our mistakes, and moving forward with a joyful heart.

THIS WEEK'S PRAYER:

Beloved God, help me grow in wisdom and humility, to listen to advice and accept discipline. It is my life's goal to be counted among the wise, but I know how long and arduous a path that is, so I seek out experts and advisors to keep growing and learning. There are many plans in my heart, but I know it is Your purpose that prevails, and I open joyfully to learn of your plans for me.

RUMINATIONS:

What plans are in your heart? It may be hard to focus on them now, but it helps our hearts and minds to look at the bigger picture and remember. Whether it's finally writing that memoir, or simply starting a "side hustle" to cover unexpected pandemic-related expenses, take a moment to take stock of what you want to accomplish:

_____

_____

_____

_____

_____

_____

What do I need to do to listen to advice and accept discipline? Who has achieved what I'm hoping to do, and how can I learn from them? Are they friends and co-workers I can call, or experts whose articles and videos I can watch? Brainstorm some ideas:

_____

_____

_____

_____

_____

_____

_____

_____

_____

_____

_____

_____

_____

_____

_____

_____

_____

_____

_____

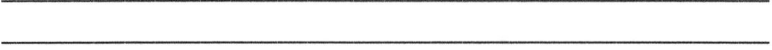

Passage 18:

JOHN 14:27

27 Peace I leave with you; my peace I give you. I do not give to you as the world gives. Do not let your hearts be troubled and do not be afraid.

THOUGHTS ON THIS PASSAGE:

There is so much important thought packed into this short passage. First, here God tells us that He gives us His peace. It is what He leaves with us.

Secondly, He does not give as this world gives. This is crucial to understand, because since we are of this world, we tend to be more attuned to things of this world. It's why we understand when someone brings us a simple birthday present but fail to see a great gift God has given us in removing an obstacle in our way or teaching us an important life lesson. The tangible makes sense to us, but God's way can sometimes be obscured to us as we look with earthly eyes.

Ultimately, this passage is about relinquishing our fear and making sure our hearts are not troubled. When we trust in God completely, we can feel nothing but peace. It is the work we'll need to come back to again and again to fully appreciate it. It is the work of a lifetime.

THIS WEEK'S PRAYER:

God, thank You for the peace You give me. Help me see Your gifts as you give them, not as the things the world gives. Please make my heart like a calm lake and take my fear from me. I relinquish my troubles and fears into your steady hands, and open to hearing Your guidance and experiencing Your love, today and always.

RUMINATIONS:

What is troubling your heart this week? We've done similar exercises before, but you'll find that as weeks wear on, new troubles come into your heart, and old ones get resolved. It is useful to revisit the things that trouble us, because sometimes with the perspective of time, we begin to see God's work in our lives. So take a moment to write your troubles afresh:

_____

_____

_____

_____

_____

_____

As we've been doing this work together, you've also uncovered some things that bring you peace. Perhaps they're a specific passage of scripture, or a small habit you've developed as a result of our work here. Look back to see which of the exercises brought you most peace. Make a list here of tools you can use when you want to get in touch with God's peace:

_____

_____

_____

_____

_____
_____
_____
_____
_____
_____
_____
_____
_____
_____
_____
_____
_____
_____
_____
_____
_____
_____
_____
_____
_____
_____

Passage 19:

REVELATION 21:4

[4]"He will wipe every tear from their eyes. There will be no more death'[a1] or mourning or crying or pain, for the old order of things has passed away."

THOUGHTS ON THIS PASSAGE:

If you've come here in mourning, this passage is for you. So much of this pandemic has been frightening and sudden and painful. Sometimes, when all of the comfort of this world escapes us, this passage reminds us of the grand sweep of God's eternal plan. One day, He will wipe every tear from our eyes and there shall be no more death. During my most difficult times, I sometimes read myself this passage over and over again. This order – the old order – will one day pass away, and the things that trouble us and fill our hearts with anguish now will be gone. There will be no more mourning or crying. If right now you're not sure how you'll ever feel renewed, remember God has a greater plan for us all.

THIS WEEK'S PRAYER:

---

1. https://www.biblegateway.com/passage/?search=Revelation+21%3A4&version=NIV#fen-NIV-31058a

God, in my despair, remind me that one day You will wipe every tear from my eyes and there shall be no more death or mourning or crying or pain. Help me hold fast and hopeful and rejoice in Your word until this painful moment passes. Remind me of the rewards of Your love, and of life everlasting.

RUMINATIONS:

Some days, nothing but keeping focused on eternal reward. I am not one to go to that reminder often, because I refuse to believe that this world is supposed to be nothing but a waiting place for the next life. I believe God wants us to experience His creation, and grow our spirits through the things of this world, while keeping fast to His word. But, some days, often the most painful days, it helps me to remember that despite the troubles of this world, one day there will be no more death, and no more mourning and despair.

Take a moment to write about the ways that this thought brings you comfort. If you're too sad and weak to even come up with your own reasons (and, let's face it, we're all there at some point), then simply copy the passage above, taking extra care on the words that bring you comfort. Circle them, rewrite them, draw them... whatever you need to do to find a moment's comfort.

_____
_____
_____
_____
_____
_____
_____

Write your own prayer to God that you can recite when you are in the worst pain. What do you need from God? What can you open to understanding?

Passage 20:

PSALM 91:1-6

He who dwells in the secret place of the Most High
will rest in the shadow of the Almighty.

^{2} I will say of the Lord, "He is my refuge and my fortress;
my God, in whom I trust."

^{3} Surely he will save you
from the fowler's snare
and from the deadly pestilence.

^{4} He will cover you with his feathers,
and under his wings you will find refuge;
his faithfulness will be your shield and rampart.

^{5} You will not fear the terror of night,
nor the arrow that flies by day,

^{6} nor the pestilence that stalks in the darkness,
nor the plague that destroys at midday.

THOUGHTS ON THIS PASSAGE:

I love so many of the Psalms, but this one resonates particularly with me during these coronavirus days. Pandemics, pestilences and plagues are nothing new to humanity. We've been dealing with them since the beginning of time. This may feel new and unexpected because it's been a hundred years since we've dealt with anything of this magnitude, but Scripture is full of references to the pandemics faced by God's people. It is scary, but it is not new. If anything, today God protects us even more because we now have access to good hygiene and to modern medicines. But the age-old shield of God's love is available to us every day we work through this frightening time.

God is our refuge and our fortress, in whom we trust. When we fear, we turn to him. This beautiful Psalm reminds us of the many ways God protects us.

THIS WEEK'S PRAYER:

For this week's prayer, instead of reciting one of our own, simply recite the above. Better yet, look up Psalm 91 in your favorite Bible (or online) and recite it to yourself (and God, of course) every day this week, and every time you feel fear.

RUMINATIONS:

How can you get the most of Psalm 91? I recommend using it as a template for writing your own prayer of faith and trust. For example, I would venture to guess you don't often fear the fowler's snare, but you may very much fear losing your job. Write your own celebration of God's might and love.

Begin it with: "surely God will save me from" and then write everything you wish to turn over to God:

_____

_____

_____

_____

_____

_____

What work that you've done in the pages of this book have brought you closest to God? In which passages have you found the most strength? How will you continue your study of Scripture and your habit of prayer? Will you go back and work through the exercises again? Find a new set for yourself? Work through this book with a prayer group? List your ideas here:

_____

_____

_____

_____

_____

_____

_____

_____

_____

_____

_____

_____

_____

_____

_____

_____

_____

_____

_____

_____

_____

_____

_____

_____

The End is Only the Beginning

THESE ARE DIFFICULT times. We don't know how long we'll be coping with this scourge. But the work you've done here is proof of your faith, resilience, and openness to growth. This is not an easy path, but it is a righteous one that leads to everlasting life. I hope you've learned new things that have made it satisfying and significant.

We can (and should!) spend a lifetime growing in our understanding of Scripture. There is such a wealth of inspiration, insight, and instruction for living in it, that we have only scratched the surface here.

Sign up for weekly inspiration and be the first to know about new devotionals and prayer journals at

http://PrudenceGraham.com

www.ingramcontent.com/pod-product-compliance
Lightning Source LLC
Chambersburg PA
CBHW032058070426
42452CB00049B/794